want—catcher

a record of pregnant writing

adra raine

the operating system c. 2018

the operating system print//document chapbook

want—catcher: a record of pregnant writing

ISBN: 978-1-946031-40-2
Library of Congress Catalog Number: 2018945768

copyright © 2018 by Adra Raine
edited and designed by Lynne DeSilva-Johnson with poetry editor Peter Milne Greiner

is released under a Creative Commons CC-BY-NC-ND (Attribution, Non Commercial, No Derivatives) License: its reproduction is encouraged for those who otherwise could not afford its purchase in the case of academic, personal, and other creative usage from which no profit will accrue. Complete rules and restrictions are available at: http://creativecommons.org/licenses/by-nc-nd/3.0/
For additional questions regarding reproduction, quotation, or to request a pdf for review contact operator@theoperatingsystem.org

This text was set in The Constellation of Heracles, Minion, Franchise, and OCR-A Standard.
Books from The Operating System are distributed to the trade by SPD/Small Press Distribution, with ePub and POD via Ingram, with production by Spencer Printing, in Honesdale, PA, in the USA.

Cover Art uses "Tulare County, California. In Farm Security Administration Camp. Mother from Oklahoma tends baby with dysentery and awaits arrival of FSA camp resident nurse," a 1939 nitrate negative from Dorothea Lange's FSA/Office of War Information holdings, in the public domain.

The operating system is a member of the Radical Open Access Collective, a community of scholar-led, not-for-profit presses, journals and other open access projects. Now consisting of 40 members, we promote a progressive vision for open publishing in the humanities and social sciences.
Learn more at: http://radicaloa.disruptivemedia.org.uk/about/

Your donation makes our publications, platform and programs possible! We <3 You.
bit.ly/growtheoperatingsystem

the operating system
141 Spencer Street #203
Brooklyn, NY 11205
www.theoperatingsystem.org
operator@theoperatingsystem.org

want-catcher

a record of pregnant writing

adra raine

WEEK 10, HOW MUCH WEIGHT A STRUCTURE HOLDS	7
WEEK 11, PAYING ATTENTION	8
WEEK 13, GENDER TROUBLE	9
WEEK 14, SOFT TISSUE	11
WEEK 15, RECENT DREAMS	12
WEEK 16, DECADES	13
WEEK 16, PLACEMAKER	15
WEEK 17, OH, YOU DON'T LOOK JEWISH	16
WEEK 18, THE WORMHOLE, CHICAGO	17
WEEK 19, LITTLE DRAMAS	18
WEEK 20, HALF WAY	20
WEEK 21, POETRY IS THE ARCHITECTURE OF LANGUAGE	21
WEEK 22, INDICIATIONS OF PAIN	22
WEEK 22, AT THE DINER IN THE CONFEDERATE TOWN	23
WEEK 23, PRENATAL YOGA	24
WEEK 24	25
WEEK 25	26
WEEK 26, WEEK 27, WEEK 28, THE WORLD IS SHIT	27
WEEK 29, SEARCH RESULTS	28
WEEKS IN BETWEEN	29
WEEK 33, BAG OF WATER	30
WEEK 34, VIABLE LIFE	31
WEEK 35, THIRTY-FIVE	32
WEEK 36, IN RETROSPECT	33
WEEK 42, NARRATIVE OF EVENTS	35

WEEK TEN
how much weight a structure holds

At week 10, the baby-to-be is about the size of a kumquat. Kumquat is even more fun to say than kidney bean. "We'd be happy anywhere—just you, me, and the kumquat." According to this week's description of "your developing baby," the spine is fully formed this week: there is a human person growing inside me.

This home structure: how my spine moves as I wash my hair, wash my body, twist under the showerhead to wash away the soap, all the trouble it's been giving me lately.

I tell Leah about the baby's spine forming this week. She adds, "It's crazy to think how it is part of you now but will eventually be this autonomous person." But this person growing inside me already seems wholly autonomous. I don't really think or feel her as part of me. It doesn't even seem accurate to say we share a body. She is inside my body, but my body inside what—the world? We live in different spaces, though we consume the same resources.

Lying in bed last night, away from home, I was staring up at the exposed beams running in three different directions to a center beam, above me—solid, heavy. I thought how this would really crush us if it came tumbling down.

"If the free-traders cannot understand how one nation can grow rich at the expense of another, we need not wonder, since these same gentlemen also refuse to understand how within one country one class can enrich itself at the expense of another."

Autonomous at whose expense?

WEEK ELEVEN

paying attention

Just before the storms came in, I watched the jungle, the huge sections of movement in the trees. Like we are under water. Birds like fish, people like crustaceans. As we were floating in the ocean, Lidia, who is also pregnant, a trimester ahead, asked if I thought the babies inside us like being in the water. "Definitely," I said, "They love it."

Which is it: The womb is a form that cradles the baby resting in it; or, the womb is a prison the baby seeks to escape. Babies don't sleep through the night when they first come out. They come from a world of endless night.

The motion of my mind is haphazard, incomplete, jagged. But this is a new practice, paying attention to what my body is paying attention to.

We have a due date now, which makes this week Week 12.

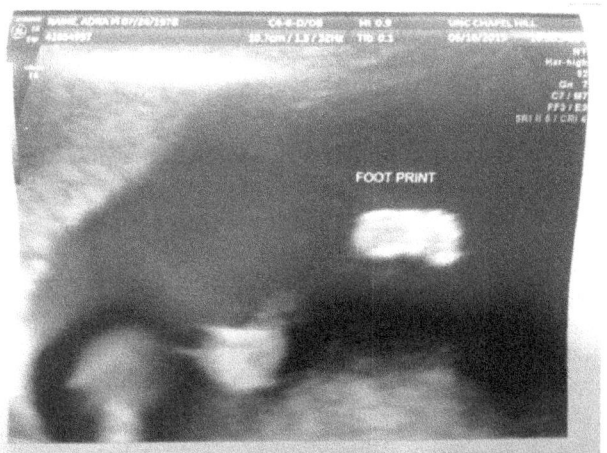

WEEK THIRTEEN
gender trouble

There are Y chromosomes in my blood.

I feel invaded?
I feel queered?
I feel subterfuged?

I feel disappointed?
I feel new?
I feel betrayed?

We wanted a girl?

I tell my therapist it is silly "to want" anything from this baby. He says, "Maybe it's silly. But so what? A lot of things are silly."

We wanted a girl. Now we want to want a boy.

What about this word: want?

A want is a mole. As in, "not much bigger than a mouse or small want." In the world of wants there is the want-catcher, want-killer, want-taker, and want-hill.

To want is to have a desire to possess or do (something). To be wanting, as in to be lacking (something).

In obsolete usage, To want is be free from (something undesirable), want coming full circle into its opposite, the snake eating its tail.

1787 J. Beattie Scoticisms 105 We wanted the plague in Scotland, when they had it in England.

We were free from a girl. We want to be free from a boy.

WEEK FOURTEEN
soft tissue

Doctors and wellness professionals, men and women, remind me how the ligaments and muscles and bones and soft tissue are loosening, they all make the same gesture with their hands, a signal that means "pulling apart." Standing for pictures outside the baptismal room—newly born wet hair oiled skin—I perceived my body in relation to father, husband, son, like a web, I am caught in, or poised in the middle of. I think: "Caught in the middle of a web," though there's some confusion in that since it is a spider's prey who is caught in a web, but the spider itself who rests in the middle. Or I didn't perceive my body in relation to father, husband, son as a web, but more like an arrangement of figures of different heights or levels in motion around my figure which was static. Or maybe their three figures were static, and mine was in motion. Perhaps it wasn't a perception as much as a note I made. My experiences over the past week are bundled together in an emotional knot that I need to pry open a little or I will explode, but it's too hot today. There are many pains in my back, hips, tailbone, butt over these past months, the primary pain rotates. New in the rotation at the end of this the longest weekend ever a spot on my lower back or right hip that feels like I've been kicked in the bone, but there is no bruise, and my recent experience suggests this pain is in the soft tissue that connects all the muscle and bone and ligament back there, there is so much soft tissue. It's pulling apart, and I feel like I've fallen on my tailbone, which every time I become conscious of or speak about recalls to mind the time when I was probably nine or ten years old and fell off the merry-go-round onto my tailbone, how I felt temporarily paralyzed, and had to go back to my friend's unfamiliar home where her mother gave me a pack of ice to sit on. Having lunch the other day at the counter, my chair tipped backward without me noticing, so that what I perceived was that the entire restaurant was sliding on its foundation. I panicked for a moment, particularly struck by the fact that no one else was reacting to this event, until the perception normalized and I understood what had happened. Now a new understanding: We were sliding around as if on the bottom of the sea, as if cradled in the womb, or trapped there, as if living under water, or held there. Did I dunk my head under the water or did he push it under? Questions I don't feel like pursuing, I've had enough loosening this week. Let's wait for the heat to break. A storm is predicted tonight.

WEEK FIFTEEN
recent dreams

I had a dream that Little Sister died. There was a big funeral parade. The autopsy report suggested that she had died from an untreated wound to the heel of one of her back legs. Homar and I looked at each other, and he said, "Well then it was our fault, we didn't take care of that when we should have." I stopped by the room in which she was being treated, when the vet realized that Little Sister had escaped. I searched for her in the stairwell. At each landing, I looked for her under a wooden bench. Finally, I spotted her and motioned to her. She slinked out from under the bench, but it wasn't her. From stage left, a giant animate stuffed tiger walked out: Little Sister. As she sat on the brick wall, I ran to her, throwing myself around her waist, happy she was alive, and wondering about her transformation.

Is this part of pregnancy? A lowered tolerance for bullshit that extends all the way down to the unconscious?

I had the dream again in which I yell at my family about capitalism. It follows the same formula as the dream in which all my friends are excluding me. Frustrated to tears.

I don't remember what I dreamed last night except that a woman's relationship to her father and brother and son is complicated by learning that her body is an object of male desire and rage.

Homar and I had our first fight. I can't remember what it was about. I remember that I was devastated, and that I thought: I'm going to be alone forever.

WEEK SIXTEEN
decades

I was a child of the 80s.

Mounir will be a child of the 20s.

My mom was a child of the 50s.

The poets I am writing about in my dissertation were children of the 40s and 50s. They were adults of the 60s and 70s. In the 80s and 90s, they were established writers, teachers, scholars. In the teens, they are subjects of dissertations.

I was a child of the 80s. I came into adulthood in the 00s. In the teens I am in my thirties.

I turned twenty in 1998. In my twenties, I lived in New York, New Jersey, Colorado, and Massachusetts.

When I met Homar he was in his twenties. I was in my thirties.

My mom is in her sixties. So is my dad.

The subjects of my dissertation are in their sixties and seventies.

Mounir is in his second trimester in the womb.

My third trimester of pregnancy will coincide with the fall semester of this coming school year in which I will be teaching one course of 19 first-year college students.

My students were children of the 00s: the decade of George W. Bush's presidency. They were born during the Clinton presidency.

I was born during the Carter presidency, but grew up in the Reagan years. I've always felt like those two years in the seventies counted for something.

Mounir will be born during the Obama presidency, but will grow up in the Clinton presidency, or perhaps the Bush presidency.

Mounir will come into adulthood in the 30s. I will be in my fifties.

The author of a cultural history of the 80s points out that it's problematic to frame historical periods by decades, requiring the scholar to do intellectual and historiographical gymnastics that are detrimental to the scholarship, i.e. they lead scholars to make stupid claims. Maybe so, but our habit of thinking in decades is just as stubborn as the fact that the earth revolves around the sun, yet we still talk of the sun rising and setting.

WEEK SIXTEEN
placemaker

too much going house under rotting from within

finish fitting and sewing help us get ready and tired
achy not tense, expanding

exponential, I believe my belly, or think I can
this one down more later

WEEK SEVENTEEN
oh, you don't look jewish

The soft cartilage is turning to bone.

I think of the bone garden in Lauren Levin's poem. Bone garden sounds like the name for something everyone knows about but me. I picture bleached bones in the southwestern sun of a Georgia O'Keefe painting.

I have developed a superstitious fear of speaking about death, including anything suggestive or associative of death, afraid it could foreshadow a miscarriage. Is this old world prudence or poetic commitment?

My attraction to the enigmatic might be an effect of ideology. E.g., the poets are the experts. Everyone knows that you're not really Jewish if your mom wasn't Jewish.

WEEK EIGHTEEN
the wormhole, chicago

    "Like A Prayer"
    "Vogue"
    "4 Minutes" feat. Justin Timberlake and Timbaland (Shazamed)
    Full-scale Delorean mounted on the wall
    Large framed oil painting of a Gremlin
    Framed photo-realistic painting of Winona Ryder in Edward Scissorhands
    First-generation Apple computer on the cream and sugar table
    "La Isla Bonita"
    Eight macbooks, including mine
    Beards, glasses, tattoos
    Baristas

Isn't this absurd consumer hipsterism a direct product of the 80s? The commodity fetish itself commoditized. But didn't the 80s also produce the critical understanding that commoditized identities are expressions of social historical forces in ideological conflict?

Everyone's getting married this summer, including me.

WEEK NINETEEN
little dramas

All the things I sometimes think I'm good at, I'm actually not very good at.

Can you entertain that all of your worst fears about yourself are true?

It takes some effort.

What if it's inconsiderate to accuse other people of inconsideration?

Lying on my back to sleep hurts my lower back. Lying on my left side hurts my ribs. Lying on my right side hurts my ribs. I can't lie on my stomach. Homar helps me build a nest of many pillows. I am learning to know pillows, how to move with them.

Homar is kept awake by chigger bites on his ankles. All night, he feels like bugs are biting him. He wakes up and itches. He gets up, looks for bugs. He wipes the sheets vigorously with his hands. Tries to sleep again. Fails. Gives up and goes to the office to read.

Pirate cries all night outside the bedroom door. He will go on for hours. We won't let him sleep with us anymore, because he sheds hair and dirt and bugs on the bed. So we let him spend the nights outside now. Homar worries about coyotes eating him. Sometimes his worry over Pirate getting eaten by coyotes keeps him awake.

> PIRATE: 1/4 wet food in morning (put it in the little oriental dishes); a half cup of dry food at night. But as he likes attention, even if bowl is already half full, he likes you to pour the new yourself on top of what's there. Pet him as much as possible; let him out, he won't stay long but likes to lie in sun and explore at night. Lots of miaowing which often doesn't mean anything. I shut door of bedroom at night so he doesn't jump up, but he may miaow in the night. The old litter stuff (he actually uses both boxes) I dump either across that Hereford st. in forest, or in our "forest" on side of goat pens, I don't think it degrades.

We met Leah at Max's house last night to pick her up to go out to celebrate having an article published and a job interview. Max's eight-year-old neighbor was playing on the roof of the shed. The little climber ignored Leah's pleading to be careful, hopping down with a smile. Homar laughed. So he did it again. Over dinner, Max told us how his neighbor spends a lot of time with him, coming into the house without knocking, opening the refrigerator, staying for dinner. He let himself in the other day while Max was on the toilet, half-naked with the door open. He told us how the child pulls clever stunts to drive a wedge between Max and Leah. I think of *The Parent Trap*.

We applied for a house rental to move into next week, since we haven't found a house to buy yet, and we have to leave here. Homar suspects the real estate agents are up to something. I woke up yesterday morning wondering about where the litter box will go.

Ebro interviewing 50 Cent: 50 Cent says a man's woman is a reflection on him. He gives examples. I roll my eyes, Homar laughs. The title of the youtube video is "Ebro pisses off 50 Cent." No real drama materializes. But anyway we are watching for 50 Cent's political economy: "He breaks down the economics of the industry really clearly."

WEEK TWENTY
halfway

Taking the week off.

WEEK TWENTYONE
poetry is the architecture of language

Starting this week, I am unambiguously pregnant. People have started asking directly: "Are you expecting?" "Are you pregnant?" Or just exclaiming: "You are pregnant!" I like it.

Two days this week, I did nothing but watch *Project Runway Season 13* and some housework. Homar reminds me: "Whenever you think you are doing nothing, you are actually growing a person inside you."

WEEK TWENTYTWO

indications of pain

Washing my hands at the kitchen sink this morning, the long horizontal cut on the top of my left hand stung and throbbed under the water. Spud got me good. It's less than two days healed. I thought how sometimes the sensation of healing is pain, that pain can be an indication of healing. Though sometimes pain can be an indication that something is wrong. Sometimes pain indicates something, or someone, is growing inside you.

Action is mobilizing this summer. I've grown wary of the appeal to outrage. Because if the spectacle of murder is more an event than structural unemployment, then aren't we operating in a framework of individual ethics that can't recognize the collective exploitation of capitalism and its colonialist tactics? If violence is the everyday condition of life, is the choice then between being permanently outraged or else cold and determined?

It is hard to gauge how tough one is. I woke up in the middle of the night last night, like the night before, with muscle spasms around my rib cage. The only way to minimize the pain was to get out of bed and walk around a bit. When I lay back down, a new pain popped up somewhere in my belly. It must have been muscle cramps, an extension of the spasms, calmed when I flex my entire body from neck to toes. But Homar asked if I was in premature labor, giving voice to my worst fear. When the second wave of pain arrived, washing over the first, I asked Homar to help me get up. I stood facing the wall and rested my forehead there as I breathed through it. I felt so much like crying, but my mom always told me that crying only makes the pain worse. Was the pain cry-worthy? Or am I wimp?

The desire to know. It isn't about whether one should or shouldn't feel outraged.

The water running over my hand stings, but also makes me feel strong.

WEEK TWENTYTWO
at the diner in the confederate town

As a pregnant woman, I can no longer be shy about my body. Most of the time I enjoy this new fact, though sometimes I am frustrated having a body that is constantly exposed, whether or not I try to conceal it. I learn that privacy is not a choice available to every body.

We get a lot of "Oh, mixed babies are so cute!" But in the surrounding towns, where we thought we might find more affordable houses, it's icy stares that seem to say, "We will drive you out of town."

WEEK TWENTYTHREE
prenatal yoga

Where are you holding on to whiteness?

Where are you holding on to capitalism?

Where are you holding on to patriarchy?

Send your breath where whiteness feels easy.

Send your breath where capitalism feels easy.

Send your breath where patriarchy feels easy.

Relax into spaces of nurturing and joy.

Relax into your discomfort: let it feel easy, hold on to it.

WEEK TWENTYFOUR

We bought a house.

WEEK TWENTYFIVE

We moved into the house we bought.

WEEK TWENTYSIX WEEK TWENTYSEVEN WEEK TWENTYEIGHT

the world is shit

I feel like I will never write again.

WEEK TWENTYNINE

search results

👍 Like   💬 Comment

Adra Raine **LST Pregnancy**
October 14, 2015 ·

About 13,500,000 results (0.02 seconds)

Showing results for when you hate everyone and **you're pregnant**
Search instead for when you hate everyone and youre pregnant

Pregnancy makes me hate everyone!!! - January 2012 Babies...
www.whattoexpect.com › Groups › January 2012 Babies › Archives ▾
Yesterday I almost posted a thread titled "today I hate everyone"! ... I then yelled out "who the eff are you staring at because I hope to god it's not my boyfriend" lol...

Pregnant and hating everyone - BabyCenter
community.babycenter.com › Birth Clubs › April 2011 Birth Club ▾
Apr 18, 2011 - Why do random strangers feel the need to give you half-a ... ed ... Pregnant and hating everyone ... When are you gonna pop that thing out?

I hate everyone - BabyCenter
community.babycenter.com › Groups › Pregnancy ▾
Aug 25, 2012 - I am 7 weeks pregnant. I am sick, tired, and I hate everyone. ... But if it gets too intense and you feel like harming yourself or someone else...

Pregnant and Miserable - TheBump.com
www.thebump.com/a/pregnant-and-miserable-prenatal-depression ▾
If you're experiencing dramatic emotional outbursts, and fits of crying and anger, Women who say they hate being pregnant may attribute their general misery to ... Sure, maybe other pregnant ladies don't mind the fact that everyone from the ...

  and 21 others   7 Comments

 Like   Comment

WEEKS IN BETWEEN

A week is not so much seven days as it is a unit measuring what to expect; a chart, a record, every week a different fruit: a measurable distance between acorn squash and squash, cabbage and honeydew, cucumber and kale, soursop and papaya; what will be missed by not writing it down.

WEEK THIRTYTHREE
bag of water

In order to protect the baby while it grows, my body has created a bag of water to surround it. More amazing than the fact that there is a tiny human swimming around inside me: where there was no bag of water, there is one now. My body made it. My body knew that it needed to make it, knew how to do it, and did it. In my culture, people get very excited about the incredible things that creatures do in nature to reproduce themselves. They make sojourns to watch sea turtles nest on the beach. They share videos on social media of cats nursing kittens and deer giving birth to fawns. But when it comes to human reproduction, they enjoy talking about the ethics of abortion and whether the fetus is a person; they like to make rules about contraception, population management, and how to intervene in third world countries. Occasionally, in movies, they produce romantic fantasies of human birth scenes. When my friend's mother learned that her daughter wanted to labor on her hands and knees, she exclaimed, "Why would you want to give birth like an animal?!"

WEEK THIRTYFOUR
viable life

I feel lighter today, after reading that if the baby were to come out now, he'd be just as OK as a full term baby.

WEEK THIRTYFIVE
thirty-five

You can count to 35 in five's, and 40 weeks is divisible by five.

The age of Advanced Maternity is 35.

I dreamt baby sticking out his hand and me taking hold of it, his little fingers wrapping around my pinky. All of him outside, while still inside, and me holding him.

We knew him by his amber eyes.

WEEK THIRTYSIX
in retrospect

I'm writing from the future, 19 months postpartum, trying to remember week 36, which was the first week of December, winter in North Carolina. It's now September, still summer hot and humid, hurricane season. All writing is a direct address to the future, or the past, typing in the dark on my phone the words I composed in my head while breastfeeding at naptime. I searched my email to be reminded that in week 36 we had a party at our house where our friends painted squares for a baby quilt my mom later sewed together. All generation is a form of time travel.

Seven generations into the future for me is

six generations into the future for you is

five generations into the future for your children is

for your children's children four generations into the future is

for your children's children's children - my great grandchildren - three generations into the future is

two generations into the future for your great grandchildren is

one generation into the future for your great grandchildren's children is

for your children's children's children's children's children's children now

WEEK FORTYTWO
narrative of events

Monday

closed soft
    over due
volumes

order time's
extension

Thursday

belly binding
bouncing

is it

    this

unclear so

    try to sleep

dream you
drive to
the beginning

in, out, on
    closed eyes
and inward
breaking

Friday

baby. baby. baby.

37

38

acknowledgements

Thank you, Lynne DeSilva-Johnson, for bringing *Want-Catcher* into the world with such care, along with all of the other projects, writers and communities you support through your incredible commitment to all of us. Thank you for providing a pathway into the beautiful and hopeful side of the messy world of publication. Thank you, too, to the whole OS team, who work so tirelessly to make this possible.

Thank you, Stephanie Young, and all of the writers in the 2015 SPT workshop who read and responded to early drafts of this writing. Thank you, poet-friends, especially Lauren Levin and Jessica Q. Stark, who encouraged me to keep going with the project. Thank you, Chris Tonelli, for inviting me to read from an early version of the manuscript at the So & So Reading Series in Raleigh, NC. Thank you, Lee-Ann Brown, for inviting me to the eclipse writing retreat at Azule in Hot Springs, NC in August 2017 where I edited the manuscript into its final form, and to Azule's director, Camille Shafer, for building such an incredible resource for artists. Thank you, Laurie Leinonen, for the painting that is part of the "Seven generations into the future" picture-poem, and to Alexis Pauline Gumbs for the writing prompt that inspired it. Thank you, Catherine Wagner, CAConrad, and Douglas Kearney, for your generosity. Thank you, Jacq Greyja, for the camaraderie.

Shout out, with all the virtual hugs, to members of the LST Pregnancy Group who know all about it. Thank you, all my dear friends, for being in it together—you are always my co-authors. Thank you, Mom, Dad, Helen, Marian, Albert, David, Eva, Samir, Sara, Ellie, Granger, and Paula for all of the love and support. Thank you, Homar, for being editor and keeping things light. Thank you, Kumquat, for generation.

poetics and process: a conversation with adra raine and lynne desilva-johnson

Greetings comrade! Thank you for talking to us about your process today! Can you introduce yourself, in a way that you would choose?

I love the spirit of being invited to "introduce yourself in a way that you would choose" as an alternative to being otherwise required to introduce ourselves in ways that we don't choose, in ways that are imposed upon us by those people, institutions, or social conventions that mediate and limit our encounters with each other. At the same time, I recognize that changing the form of introduction does not in itself change the structure of U.S. Empire in which we encounter one another, such that I still feel like I can make a right or wrong choice here, since I might only get this one chance to meet you, and we live in such urgent times, I fear that if I don't convey the right codes, many of you will lose patience with me, cross me off the list of potential community members, and move on, without me.

This anxious reaction I'm having to your generous invitation reminds of the way my students often respond when I tell them that they can complete their assignments in any compositional form they choose, in order to move them away from the often-stifling conventions of the standard college "paper," to validate and nurture the various forms of reading, thinking and expression each student brings to the table. They've told me that they are left wondering what it is I really want, certain that despite the rhetoric of freedom, there is nonetheless a correct and incorrect way to complete the assignment, with their grades, and in turn their economic futures at stake. So, I have to prove to them that they can take risks without fear of punishment (in the form of a "bad" grade), while trying at the same time to prepare them for the risks we'll need to take together to fight for transformation, without any guarantee, shifting the stakes from individual security to collective care. What is at stake in my introduction to you all? It follows a similar trajectory. I want you to read my book. I want you to like me. I want a job. I want to tell you what I'm into in case you want to talk about the things I do and work on. I want to tell you things that might contextualize my writing. I want to represent the OS in a way that won't disappoint the people who took a chance on me by accepting my manuscript. I don't want to do this alone. I want to connect. I want to open things up to look at them together. I don't want to fail. But I don't want to be afraid either. I don't want a guarantee. I want to try this out—answering your question in this polemical way. I want to make everything, including my failures, available for our collective analysis. We want things to change.

I'm Adra Raine, I'm a writer and teacher living in Durham, NC. I grew up in Boulder, CO and lived in New Jersey, New York, Massachusetts, and Maine before moving to North Carolina in 2010 to do my PhD. Right now I'm working on a dissertation on the works of Nathaniel Mackey, Ed Roberson, and Susan Howe in the 1980s-90s while teaching writing and literature at UNC-Chapel Hill. I'm currently working on a manuscript about parenthood in late capitalism titled Wonder Weeks, *of which* Want-Catcher *is the first chapter. I have a closet full of super-8 film footage that one day I hope to edit into a series of short films to add to the small handful I've finished. I own an iPhone. I watch a lot of television shows. I listen to music on Spotify. I wake up around 6am to nurse my toddler who starts our day about 45 minutes later, so I'm very sleepy by about 8pm every night. I'm currently taking a break from social media except for tracking events and local b/s/t posts. I'm an introvert, but as a Leo, I want everyone to love me. I'm still an INFP (I thought maybe I wasn't anymore).*

I don't believe or not believe in astrology and the Meyer-Briggs personality types, but in my culture they are part of how we understand ourselves. I still struggle with the residual effects of the internalized misogyny I've spent much of my thirties throwing off. I grew up in an upwardly mobile middle-to-upper-middle class home in the 1980s in a hippie town where I attended a progressive, multicultural, bilingual school that I was surprised to discover was not representative of the world, or even of the town, but was "experimental." I worked for seven years in "non-profit" contemporary art spaces, where I met a lot of great people and learned to be suspicious of cultural institutions. I avoid and resist forms of competition that pit one person's livelihood or wellbeing against another. This is a struggle when you live in the belly of global capitalism. My writing and ideas are not copyrighted.

Why are you a poet/writer/artist?

First, as a way to process experience. For me, writing, filmmaking, and artmaking are mediums for observation and reflection. I look and feel around through them, think and ask questions with them. I consider artmaking a tool that doesn't really have any special significance as an activity on its own. I don't relate to artmaking as a rarefied activity, though it's hard not to come to think of it that way, living in a culture in which art is understood primarily as an exchangeable good, both as a commodity and as cultural capital. Second, I am a poet/writer/artist in order to share, connect, and contribute to our social or collective processing of experience, observation, reflection, etc. It's a form of conversation, because conversation is another way that I/we examine and make choices in the world—sitting on the front porch with my friends at night, talking it out, or reading a book of poems someone else wrote, talking it in.

When did you decide you were a poet/writer/artist (and/or: do you feel comfortable calling yourself a poet/writer/artist, what other titles or affiliations do you prefer/feel are more accurate)?

Growing up in a household in which art and writing were folded into daily life, I found myself often recognized by others as a writer/artist and was fine with that. In college in New Jersey in the late 1990s I majored in studio art and English, with an unofficial minor in creative writing. I ran a community life-drawing class, re-ignited the campus art club, and was the student manager of the university art galleries—so I was into it. But my encounter with the art world of New York City really turned me off—I couldn't submit to the pressure to define oneself as an "artist" in order to market one's work/self. As a writer, my confidence was rattled when I became enthralled to an older novelist whose misogyny really seeped into my own sense of self and I found myself contorting my strange, speculative fiction to the masculine "realism" of Hemingway, Carver, and Cheever.

So, I felt uncomfortable for a long time calling myself an artist or a writer. It wasn't until graduate school when I became friends with generous artists and writers that I began to play with identifying as a poet and filmmaker. One of my friends was particularly committed to introducing me that way, and I recognized her gesture as a deliberate and political one, made out of care for me and for a more inclusive culture. I really admire and am grateful to her for that, and I try to emulate that practice now.

What's a "poet" (or "writer" or "artist") anyway? What do you see as your cultural and social role (in the literary / artistic / creative community and beyond)?

Another reason that I am more comfortable now calling myself a writer and an artist is that I've let go (not completely of course) of the notion of the artist as an exclusive vocation, a title one earns by passing certain tests of talent, genius, success, productivity, CV lines, sales, and so forth. I think this idea of the artist and of art is very much tied to ideologies of empire and capitalism, as they coalesce monstrously in the particularity of American ideology: e.g. American exceptionalism, possessive individualism, and the American Dream.

The cultural and social role of the artist/writer who wants to work against these ideologies is, I think, to see and articulate the structure, to re-vision the landscape of images and the architecture of language that holds and reproduces it, to dream alternatives, and to bring us together to do that work. The art we make provides a place to start, or to reflect, to plan, or to reconsider.

Talk about the process or instinct to move these poems (or your work in general) as independent entities into a body of work. How and why did this happen? Have you had this intention for a while? What encouraged and/or confounded this (or a book, in general) coming together? Was it a struggle? Did you envision this collection as a collection or understand your process as writing or making specifically around a theme while the poems themselves were being written / the work was being made? How or how not?

I feel most anchored when I have a regular writing practice, which isn't always easy to sustain. In the summer of 2014, I was reading for my PhD exams and needed some structure to facilitate poetry-writing—otherwise, it just seemed like there was never time. I signed up for a poetry workshop with Anne Boyer, whose work I was devouring at the time, hosted through Small Press Traffic (SPT). Weekly reading and writing prompts, discussion and work-shopping was really working for me, got me back into the groove. The next summer, when I was a few weeks pregnant, I joined another SPT workshop led by Stephanie Young. So, I had these two structuring principles shaping the writing: the weekly reading/writing prompts Stephanie assigned, and the weeks of pregnancy, which are at once medical categories (the belly should measure xcm at week x, you can expect y changes in your body at week y, etc.) and a kind of common language in the world of pregnancy ("How many weeks are you?").

There are charts that tell you the size of the fetus by comparing it to other objects, like fruits—at week 7, the size of a blueberry, at week 20, a banana, at week 39, the predictable watermelon. Each week I produced pages of writing. I wasn't sure if it would be a book or not, or what these writings would look like once I shaped them. I put them aside for a while, as I continued writing different kinds of poems through the first year of parenthood. I liked what I was writing and felt finally I wanted, in general, to start sharing my work with other people, but had never put a manuscript together. Since the pregnancy writing was already held together in its form, it felt like a project that I could finish and send out. I had just enough distance to edit it while still feeling connected to the place from which it was written. I tried to lift out what seemed most central in each week's writing, without losing that sense of the diarist's stream-of-consciousness. I had to resist the desire to correct my former self, to shape her into what seems to my current self a better or ideal version.

What formal structures or other constrictive practices (if any) do you use in the creation of your work? Have certain teachers or instructive environments, or readings/writings/work of other creative people informed the way you work/write?

After the two workshops with SPT, I took two workshops with Hoa Nguyen, who runs these amazing courses out of her home in Toronto with a call-in option for folks who aren't local. The meetings were on Sunday afternoons—I'd light a candle and close the door to the office while my husband hung out with the baby for two hours, occasionally entering the room quietly to breastfeed. I like workshops because they go on the google calendar, and because they push me to play with form, to form my writing into poems. The encouragement I've received in those spaces from writers I admire has also been really important. The poet Lauren Levin, who was in both SPT workshops with me and was sharing work with us every week that was blowing my mind, was one of the first people who got what I was doing and told me to keep going.

More generally, living with a child has imposed structure and routine on my daily life that has removed what previously got in the way of writing—I don't have time any more for anxiety about it, no time for hesitation. So, I write a lot more regularly now.

My biggest influences are my friends—we read other people's work together, and each other's work, and talk, talk, talk. It's harder to trace, the way living together changes us individually and in relation, you don't notice yourself or those close to you growing. You need some document of the past for comparison in order to see it.

The work I most connect to is, I think, really different from my own. It's nice to check out writing that people suggest is similar, but I usually get a little bored by it. That used to trouble me, because it suggests that I'm not really interested in my own kind of work. But I think that makes sense. Why would you seek Sameness? At the same time, I think the reasons I like the work I do describes what motivates my own writing practice.

I like work that is engaged in careful observation, plays with language as a dynamic medium for thought, analyzes and critiques the social world. I like work that gives me that feeling that the world is shit but that living is wonderful and exciting, work that makes me want to scream and dance. Here's a list: Nathaniel Mackey, Ed Roberson, Anne Boyer, Vanessa Angélica Villarreal, M.I.A., Ana Božičević, Wilson Harris, Édouard Glissant, Fredric Jameson, Angela Davis, Sun Ra, CAConrad, Le Tigre, Simon J. Ortiz, Gwendolyn Brooks, Theresa Hak Kyung Cha, Catherine Wagner, Lauryn Hill, Douglas Kearney, Susan Howe, Erica Hunt, Emily Dickinson, Alexis Pauline Gumbs.

Speaking of monikers, what does your title represent? How was it generated? Talk about the way you titled the book, and how your process of naming (individual pieces, sections, etc) influences you and/or colors your work specifically.

An unborn child is a lightning rod for so much cultural baggage. From the very beginning, deciding to become pregnant—talking to family and friends about it, going to the OB/GYN for a consultation, visiting the alternative birth center for a tour—I entered this structure that was so ideologically saturated, it was really intense. Because I was thirty-five years old when I got pregnant, I fell into the category of Advanced Maternity Age, which qualified me for free genetic testing that screens for chromosome problems early in the pregnancy. As a side effect, the test also reveals the sex of the baby—if there are any Y-chromosomes in your blood that weren't there before, it means your baby is carrying them: "a boy." There are so many things to say about this kind of testing, but I'll skip past that to say that I opted in. We were driving when we got the phone call telling us that our "numbers" were "good." The nurse asked if we wanted to know the sex. We said, Sure. And she said: It's a boy. We were surprised to find ourselves disappointed. We'd been talking about the baby as a "she." That week I wrote about the implications of this experience, recognizing the desires and fears that we were projecting onto this child—my husband and I, and the wider culture of which we are a part. When you tell someone you are pregnant, one of the most common questions people ask is about the sex of the baby. If you don't know yet, then they ask, What do you want? It's so common that you stop being weirded-out by it—you come to understand that when you live in a culture in which children are cordoned off from the adult world, and parenting is considered a private endeavor, there's no common public discourse about pregnancy and babies, people just don't know what to say. But I started thinking about this question and the word, "want." As a graduate student at a research university, I have easy access to the online OED (which is otherwise behind a pay wall). I found two unexpected definitions, one is a creature called a want, which is a small mole, and related compounds: want-catcher, want-killer, want-taker, and want-hill. I also found an obsolete definition that means to desire to be free of something. Like to be free of all the fear and desire this child was already holding for all of us. A want-catcher is, I presume, someone whose job it is to trap the unwanted creature. But I hear an echo of dream-catcher in it too. Dream or want. The child as a want-catcher. Pregnancy as a want-catcher. Poetry as a want-catcher. I don't know if Want-Catcher is about all of this exactly, but I think it registers that sense of the structure of feeling that life in late capitalism produces, what Douglas Kearney calls "an uneasiness" in the thoughtful and generous blurb he wrote for the book.

The titles always come last but in turn often provoke further revision. I play around with them a lot, to see what resonances they produce, and often learn a lot about the poem that way.

What does this particular work represent to you as indicative of your method/creative practice? your history? your mission/intentions/hopes/plans?

I've grown increasingly skeptical of aesthetic pleasure that derives from the satisfying turn of phrase, the profound insight, and other forms of "getting it right." Because the world is not right. I want my work to register that not-rightness.

Sometimes when I'm teaching a class, I'll find myself in this mode of ecstatic enthusiasm, because I'm so excited that we are onto something, when the students and I are breaking through something. But there's this kind of icky feeling that follows—a sense of having lost track of what-we-still-don't-get. The difference between joy that is productive and joy that makes living in the status quo more comfortable is not at all easy to discern. Susan Howe has this line that I repeat a lot: "Rungs between escape and enclosure are confusing and compelling."

For the sake of ego, I want people to read my work and say, "I like it! It's great! It's beautiful!" But in terms of what I really care about, which is for things to change, it's important to examine what people's reactions—positive and negative—represent and suggest about what is at stake. Sometimes it's not good that they like it, sometimes it's very good that they don't.

All of that is to say that when editing the manuscript for Want-Catcher *I tried to let go of my instinct to please people (particular or imagined). I wanted to make something true. I don't think it's beautiful or brilliant or ground-breaking, or any of those things that I've internalized art is supposed to be in order to be of value.*

I think the aestheticizing of politics, as Walter Benjamin theorized in a different but related context, is something we have to be really cautious about participating in. He warned that fascism gives people the right of expression without giving them the right to change property relations. In other words, "the logical outcome of fascism," he writes, "is an aestheticizing of political life." This book represents to some degree the kind of work I make when I am attuned to this threat.

On a personal level, it represents me letting go finally, putting my work out there, as they say.

What does this book DO (as much as what it says or contains)?

I'm not sure yet.

What would be the best possible outcome for this book? What might it do in the world, and how will its presence as an object facilitate your creative role in your community and beyond? What are your hopes for this book, and for your practice?

The best possible outcome for the book is that someone reads it and it means something to them. Maybe it articulates something they've been thinking about or feeling or experiencing, or provides a contrast against which they can articulate those things differently than I have, or comes into dialogue with different thoughts, feeling, experiences of theirs. That it gets to participate in a conversation somewhere.

The best possible outcome for me personally, as the author of the book, is that it connects me to people, that people would reach out to talk to me about their reading of it or anything else, and share their work with me.

Let's talk a little bit about the role of poetics and creative community in social activism, in particular in what I call "Civil Rights 2.0," which has remained immediately present all around us in the time leading up to this series' publication. I'd be curious to hear some thoughts on the challenges we face in speaking and publishing across lines of race, age, privilege, social/cultural background, and sexuality within the community, vs. the dangers of remaining and producing in isolated "silos."

I've been trying to articulate this cultural shift that I think we are living through, which in the broadest terms I describe as a shift from aesthetics to politics in our judgment of art. That's a tricky way to put it, because those terms—aesthetics, politics, art—can be pretty misleading, particularly when they mean different things to different people and separating them may signal a philosophy of art that has taken on various politics over its history. But what I'm trying to respond to are things like this: When Beyoncé released Lemonade *in 2016, the debates people had about it were predominantly around political questions: Is Beyoncé a good feminist or a bad feminist? Is she a black radical or a sellout? Is she an activist or a capitalist? While these questions were tied to traditionally "aesthetic" questions about the album's form, analyses of the lyrics, responses to the musical production, identifying artistic influences, and so forth, even these were aimed ultimately at making a political judgment about the work. In other words, the dominant value judgment—the answer to the question, Is it good, or bad?—has become a matter of evaluating whether the art expresses good or bad politics.*

This moment would appear to finally make those debates over whether or how art is political officially irrelevant. But I see a new problem emerging, as the shift from aesthetics to politics runs the risk of aestheticizing politics as Benjamin warned us about—such that the difference between "good or bad politics" becomes merely a matter of personal expression as opposed to social effects or outcomes. Because when the outcome always seems the same, which is that nothing changes—the powerful become more powerful, the war machine grows, the tools of exploitation continue to innovate—then "politics," which is about the action of change, becomes inert, merely a container for ethical concepts and moralism. Benjamin theorized that the opposite formula—the politicization of art—was communism's necessary strategy on the cultural front. But how do we discern the difference?

The turnaround time between the politicization of art and its cooption into its opposite is so fast that we hardly have time to keep up. Overnight we see our politics turned into mere matters of style used by the dominant ideology to sell commodities like Pepsi and mobile apps, to sell ideas like diversity and liberal progress. So, we have to stay ahead of that, have to keep checking in on whose agenda our art is serving and what effect it is producing. And it's hard: "Rungs between escape and enclosure are confusing and compelling." The question that moves then to the foreground is one about strategy and organization. How to keep in circulation the voices of people who are shouting out the truth about what is happening, how to reach each other through all of these layers of capitalist mediation. Small presses and the Internet have been an important answer, but I think even those spaces, despite our best efforts, are getting pretty thoroughly consumed by the blob that intrudes on our encounters and silences us by taking away our ability to hear each other. Particularly in the way we see all of these self-selecting micro-communities, or isolated "silos" as you put it. In a 2014 interview, the musician Anthony Braxton responds to a comment about how online communities don't facilitate the kind of tension that cultivates change: "If you like polkas and you go to the Internet and find people who like polkas, you're with a group that feels the same way you feel. The Internet, which is so incredible for all the possibilities it's given us, also gives us the possibility to find kindred spirits in every domain. So, this concept of tension is really a wonderful way to talk about this. There's no tension when everybody agrees." Under these conditions, I think we are in the process of shifting strategies. I'm not sure exactly what it looks like or where it is located. I think right now there's a tension between the energy that is going into building the social relations that we want to be in practice when the revolution comes and the energy that is going into mass organizing that has to compromise in order to build the numbers we need to bring on the revolution. Can we make this tension productive? And how do we revolutionize the notion of "revolution" in an era of globally militarized capital? Where is the cultural front when aesthetics gives way to politics? Is "art" as a category necessary or even relevant to what we are trying to do, what we have to do?

So, I have a lot of questions, but my answer to your question is that if the primary role of the creative community is to facilitate tensions that cultivate change, the challenge is to outrun those forces—external and internal—that render the politics of our art ineffective, to not let those tensions be obfuscated either by repressing them under silos of consensus or by emphasizing them as a battle of morals, but to keep them active and dynamic.

Is there anything else we should have asked, or that you want to share?

These questions were so great—I appreciate the way you provoked me to consider both my ideas about art making in general and the chapbook in particular. There's more consistency between the two than I thought! It has helped me understand myself as a writer/artist, the things I already have a very strong sense of and commitment to and the uncertainties I'm still working through and shaky on. I'm really grateful. Thank you!

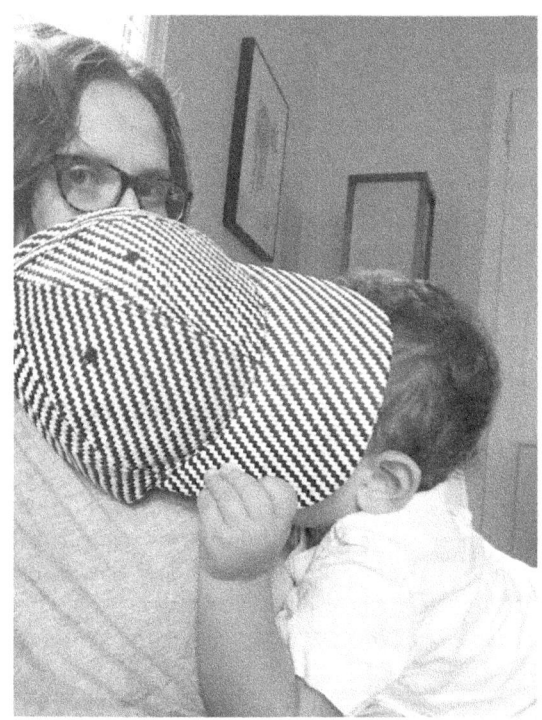

ADRA RAINE is a writer living in Durham, NC. She is a PhD candidate at the University of North Carolina at Chapel Hill where she teaches literature and writing and is completing a dissertation on contemporary U.S. poetry titled *Resonance Over Resolution: Resisting Definition in Nathaniel Mackey, Ed Roberson, and Susan Howe's Post-1968 Poetics*. Otherwise, she is working on a book length manuscript of poems and prose about parenthood in late capitalism titled *Wonder Weeks,* of which *Want-Catcher* is the first chapter.

WHY PRINT DOCUMENT?

The Operating System uses the language "print document" to differentiate from the book-object as part of our mission to distinguish the act of documentation-in-book-FORM from the act of publishing as a backwards-facing replication of the book's agentive *role* as it may have appeared the last several centuries of its history. Ultimately, I approach the book as TECHNOLOGY: one of a variety of printed documents (in this case, bound*) that humans have invented and in turn used to archive and disseminate ideas, beliefs, stories, and other evidence of production.*

Ownership and use of printing presses and access to (or restriction of printed materials) has long been a site of struggle, related in many ways to revolutionary activity and the fight for civil rights and free speech all over the world. While (in many countries) the contemporary quotidian landscape has indeed drastically shifted in its access to platforms for sharing information and in the widespread ability to "publish" digitally, even with extremely limited resources, the importance of publication on physical media has not diminished. In fact, this may be the most critical time in recent history for activist groups, artists, and others to insist upon learning, establishing, and encouraging personal and community documentation practices. Hear me out.

With The OS's print endeavors I wanted to open up a conversation about this: the ultimately radical, transgressive act of creating PRINT /DOCUMENTATION in the digital age. It's a question of the archive, and of history: who gets to tell the story, and what evidence of our life, our behaviors, our experiences are we leaving behind? We can know little to nothing about the future into which we're leaving an unprecedentedly digital document trail — but we can be assured that publications, government agencies, museums, schools, and other institutional powers that be will continue to leave BOTH a digital and print version of their production for the official record. Will we?

As a (rogue) anthropologist and long time academic, I can easily pull up many accounts about how lives, behaviors, experiences — how THE STORY of a time or place — was pieced together using the deep study of correspondence, notebooks, and other physical documents which are no longer the norm in many lives and practices. As we move our creative behaviors towards digital note taking, and even audio and video, what can we predict about future technology that is in any way assuring that our stories will be accurately told – or told at all? How will we leave these things for the record?

In these documents we say: WE WERE HERE, WE EXISTED, WE HAVE A DIFFERENT STORY

- Lynne DeSilva-Johnson, Founder/Managing Editor,
THE OPERATING SYSTEM, Brooklyn NY 2017

SELECTED RECENT AND FORTHCOMING OS PRINT/DOCUMENTS

Ark Hive-Marthe Reed [2019]
A Bony Framework for the Tangible Universe-D. Allen [kin(d)*, 2019]
Śnienie / Dreaming - Marta Zelwan/Krystyna Sakowicz,
(Polish-English/dual-language) trans. Victoria Miluch [glossarium, 2019]
Opera on TV-James Brunton [kin(d)*, 2019]
Alparegho: Pareil-À-Rien / Alparegho, Like Nothing Else - Hélène Sanguinetti
(French-English/dual-language), trans. Ann Cefola [glossarium, 2019]
Hall of Waters-Berry Grass [kin(d)*, 2019]
High Tide Of The Eyes - Bijan Elahi (Farsi-English/dual-language)
trans. Rebecca Ruth Gould and Kayvan Tahmasebian [glossarium, 2019]
I Made for You a New Machine and All it Does is Hope - Richard Lucyshyn [2019]
Illusory Borders-Heidi Reszies [2019]
Transitional Object-Adrian Silbernagel [kin(d)*, 2019]
A Year of Misreading the Wildcats [2019]

An Absence So Great and Spontaneous It Is Evidence of Light - Anne Gorrick [2018]
The Book of Everyday Instruction - Chloe Bass [2018]
Executive Orders Vol. II - a collaboration with the Organism for Poetic Research [2018]
One More Revolution - Andrea Mazzariello [2018]
The Suitcase Tree - Filip Marinovich [2018]
Chlorosis - Michael Flatt and Derrick Mund [2018]
Sussuros a Mi Padre - Erick Sáenz [2018]
Sharing Plastic - Blake Nemec [2018]
The Book of Sounds - Mehdi Navid (Farsi dual language, trans. Tina Rahimi) [2018]
In Corpore Sano : Creative Practice and the Challenged Body [Anthology, 2018];
Lynne DeSilva-Johnson and Jay Besemer, co-editors
Abandoners - Lesley Ann Wheeler [2018]
Jazzercise is a Language - Gabriel Ojeda-Sague [2018]
Return Trip / Viaje Al Regreso - Israel Dominguez;
(Spanish-English dual language) trans. Margaret Randall [2018]
Born Again - Ivy Johnson [2018]
Attendance - Rocío Carlos and Rachel McLeod Kaminer [2018]
Singing for Nothing - Wally Swist [2018]
The Ways of the Monster - Jay Besemer [2018]
Walking Away From Explosions in Slow Motion - Gregory Crosby [2018]
The Unspoken - Bob Holman [Bowery Books imprint - 2018]
Field Guide to Autobiography - Melissa Eleftherion [2018]
Kawsay: The Flame of the Jungle - María Vázquez Valdez
(Spanish-English dual language) trans. Margaret Randall [2018]

OS PRINT DOCUMENT ANNUAL CHAPBOOK SERIES TITLES

CHAPBOOK SERIES 2018 : TALES
Greater Grave - Jacq Greyja; Needles of Itching Feathers - Jared Schlickling;
Want-Catcher - Adra Raine; We, The Monstrous - Mark DuCharme

CHAPBOOK SERIES 2017 : INCANTATIONS
featuring original cover art by Barbara Byers
sp. - Susan Charkes; Radio Poems - Jeffrey Cyphers Wright;
Fixing a Witch/Hexing the Stitch - Jacklyn Janeksela;
cosmos a personal voyage by carl sagan ann druyan steven sotor and me - Connie Mae Oliver

CHAPBOOK SERIES 2016: OF SOUND MIND
*featuring the quilt drawings of Daphne Taylor
Improper Maps - Alex Crowley; While Listening - Alaina Ferris;
Chords - Peter Longofono; Any Seam or Needlework - Stanford Cheung

CHAPBOOK SERIES 2015: OF SYSTEMS OF
*featuring original cover art by Emma Steinkraus
Cyclorama - Davy Knittle; The Sensitive Boy Slumber Party Manifesto - Joseph
Cuillier; Neptune Court - Anton Yakovlev; Schema - Anurak Saelow

CHAPBOOK SERIES 2014: BY HAND
Pull, A Ballad - Maryam Parhizkar;
Can You See that Sound - Jeff Musillo
Executive Producer Chris Carter - Peter Milne Greiner;
Spooky Action at a Distance - Gregory Crosby;

CHAPBOOK SERIES 2013: WOODBLOCK
*featuring original prints from Kevin William Reed
Strange Coherence - Bill Considine; The Sword of Things - Tony Hoffman;
Talk About Man Proof - Lancelot Runge / John Kropa;
An Admission as a Warning Against the Value of Our Conclusions -Alexis Quinlan

DOC U MENT
/däkyəmənt/

First meant "instruction" or "evidence," whether written or not.

noun - a piece of written, printed, or electronic matter that provides information or evidence or that serves as an official record
verb - record (something) in written, photographic, or other form
synonyms - paper - deed - record - writing - act - instrument

[Middle English, precept, from Old French, from Latin *documentum*, example, proof, from *docre*, to teach; see *dek-* in Indo-European roots.]

Who is responsible for the manufacture of value?

Based on what supercilious ontology have we landed in a space where we vie against other creative people in vain pursuit of the fleeting credibilities of the scarcity economy, rather than freely collaborating and sharing openly with each other in ecstatic celebration of MAKING?

While we understand and acknowledge the economic pressures and fear-mongering that threatens to dominate and crush the creative impulse, we also believe that **now more than ever we have the tools to relinquish agency via cooperative means,** fueled by the fires of the Open Source Movement.

Looking out across the invisible vistas of that rhizomatic parallel country we can begin to see our community beyond constraints, in the place where intention meets
resilient, proactive, collaborative organization.

Here is a document born of that belief, sown purely of imagination and will.
When we document we assert. We print to make real, to reify our being there.
When we do so with mindful intention to address our process, to open our work to others,
to create beauty in words in space, to respect and acknowledge the strength of the page we now hold physical, a thing in our hand… we remind ourselves that, like Dorothy: *we had the power all along, my dears.*

THE PRINT! DOCUMENT SERIES
is a project of
the trouble with bartleby
in collaboration with
the operating system

www.ingramcontent.com/pod-product-compliance
Lightning Source LLC
Chambersburg PA
CBHW081339080526
44588CB00017B/2684